Art Smart

PRINT IT!

Traci Bunkers

QEB

QEB Publishing

Editor: Lauren Taylor
Design: Tall Tree Ltd www.talltreebooks.co.uk
Illustrator: Tom Connell

Copyright © QED Publishing 2012

Published in the United States by
QEB Publishing, Inc.
3 Wrigley, Suite A
Irvine, CA 92618

www.qed-publishing.co.uk

A CIP record for this book is available from the
Library of Congress.

ISBN 978 1 60992 277 1

Printed in China

Picture credits
(t=top, b=bottom, l=left, r=right, c=centre, fc=front cover, bc=back cover)
Mark Winwood: 5br, 11br, 15br
Philip Wilkins: 7br, 9br, 13br, 17br, 19br, 21br, 23br, 25br, 27br
Shutterstock: fctc, tr, bccl, tr Beata Becla; fcc, bctc Irina Nartova;
3tl, 16br, 26br George Filyagin; 3br, 6tr, 19br Nattika; 6br, 28l
Africa Studio; 8tr, 22cl Picsfive; 8br discpicture; 10c oksana2010;
11bl magicoven; 12tr, 19tr artproem; 20tc Kazyavka; 21tr
FrameAngel; 21c Africa Studio; 26tr, 29tr magicoven; 28tr
Anteromite

Note to adults:
Some children might be able to
do some or all of these projects
on their own, while others might
need more help. These are
projects that you can work on
together, not only to avoid any
problems or accidents, but also
to share in the fun of making art.

At the top of the page for each project you will
find this handy key. It will tell you the difficulty
level to expect from each project:

Quick Creative Fix
These projects are quick, easy and perfect for
a beginner.

Sharpen Your Skills
Confident with your beginner skills? Move onto
these slightly tougher projects.

Ready For a Challenge
For a challenging project you can really get
stuck into.

Creative Masterpiece
Think you can tackle the toughest printing
projects? Have a go at these.

CONTENTS

PRINTED PET T-SHIRT

You can liven up plain T-shirts with this easy printing method.

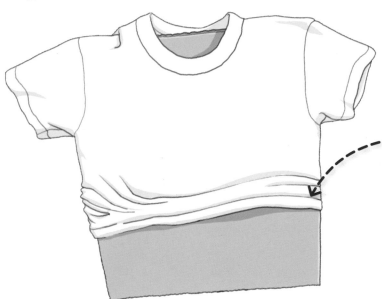

1 Insert a piece of cardboard or folded newspapers inside the T-shirt. This will stop the paint soaking through to the back. Make sure the shirt is smooth and not wrinkled.

2 Squeeze some paint onto your paint palette, then use a sponge brush to spread it into a thin layer. Use several colors for a more vibrant design.

3 Draw a picture of your pet, or a favorite animal, into the paint with a paintbrush. Everything will print backwards, so if you include any writing, be sure to write it backwards.

4 Carefully place the painted side of the paint palette on the T-shirt where you want the design to print. Press down on the palette to be sure the whole picture will print.

5 Carefully peel the palette off the T-shirt and let the paint dry. Heat set the design according to the directions on the fabric paint.

Practice your design on paper first to get the best outcome!

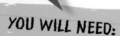

PICTURE PERFECT

Decorate a picture frame with stamps you can make and change yourself!

1 Pour a small amount of light colored paint into the plastic cup. Paint the front and sides of the frame with the paint. Let it dry.

2 Roll a small piece of modeling clay into a short log shape. Pinch one end to make a small handle and flatten the other end for the stamp.

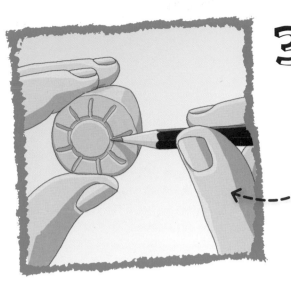

3 Use a pencil to draw a design into the flat part of the stamp. You could also make a texture by pressing different items into the clay, such as a straw or the pattern on the sole of a shoe.

4 Squeeze a small amount of paint onto the sponge. Use your fingers to spread it around. Press the stamp onto the paint on the sponge, then stamp onto the frame. Repeat to create whatever pattern you like.

5 When the frame is dry, you can stamp the frame again using a different color or design.

This would make a unique gift!

COOL KID SHOES

Impress everyone with these arty shoes that you painted yourself.

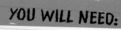

1 Stuff the shoes with scrunched-up newspaper so that they hold their shape. Apply the masking tape to make a stripy pattern on the shoes.

2 Squeeze a small amount of paint onto a paper plate. Dip the paintbrush into the paint, then tap the brush between the masking tape stripes to color in the spaces.

3 When the paint is dry, remove the masking tape.

4 Place the stickers onto the unpainted areas of the shoes. Using a different paint color, tap the paintbrush around the edges of the stickers, coloring in the stripes.

5 When the paint is dry, remove the stickers. Add some decoration with fabric pens or color in the white shapes, if you like.

Add some funky laces to make your shoes even more colorful.

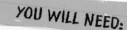

ARTIST'S SELF-PORTRAIT

Every artist should make a self-portrait, and printing gives you a unique way to do it!

YOU WILL NEED:

- Large piece of cardboard
- Scissors
- Sheet of paper
- White glue, in a squeeze bottle
- Thick yarn or string
- Acrylic paint
- Plastic cup
- Sponge brush
- Crayons, marker pens and glitter glue

1 Cut your cardboard a little smaller than your piece of paper. Draw your self-portrait onto the cardboard using a felt-tip pen.

2 Trace over the lines of your self-portrait drawing with white glue, then press the thick yarn or string into the glue. Let the glue dry.

3 Pour a small amount of paint into the plastic cup. Dip your sponge brush into the paint, then brush it onto the glued yarn.

4 Before the paint dries, place your paper on top of the self-portrait. With your hands, push down on the paper, carefully moving your hands around so that the paint prints onto the paper.

5 Lift the paper off the printing cardboard and let the paint dry. Decorate your printed portrait with things like crayons, marker pens and glitter glue.

You can use this method to create a picture of anything you like!

WICKED WRAPPING PAPER

Printing is great for creating repeating patterns—perfect for making your own wrapping paper!

YOU WILL NEED:

- Marker pen
- Adhesive craft foam
- Scissors
- Empty cardboard juice can
- Masking tape
- Poster paint, in various colors
- Paint palette
- Sponge brush
- A large sheet of paper

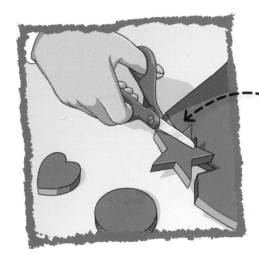

1 Draw some simple shapes, such as stars, hearts and zigzags, on the craft foam. Cut the shapes out with scissors.

2 Ask an adult to tape the lid back onto the can with masking tape. This will help it hold its shape.

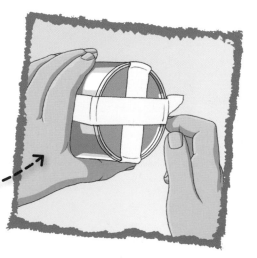

3 Stick the foam shapes onto the can, leaving an inch free at each end for rolling with your hands.

4 Squeeze some paint onto your paint palette. Apply the paint onto the foam shapes with the sponge brush.

5 Roll the can over the paper, printing the foam shapes pattern. Apply more paint when you need to. When the paint is dry, use a different color to print on top of the first layer.

You can make so many different designs with this method!

TERRIFIC TREASURE BOX

Transform a simple box into a colorful treasure box to store all your odds and ends.

1 Paint the box and lid one color.

2 Draw some simple shapes onto the pop-up sponges with a pencil, then cut them out with scissors.

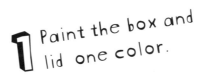

3 Place the sponge shapes in water to let them expand. Then squeeze the water out of them. You won't need to do this if you're using normal sponge or foam.

4 Pour a small amount of paint onto your palette. Dip the sponge stamps into the paint so that the bottom surface is covered, then stamp it onto the box or lid. Stamp your box with different colors and stamps to make the pattern you want.

5 When the paint is dry, you can decorate your box with crayons, marker pens, glitter glue or anything else you'd like.

You can decorate the inside of the treasure box too!

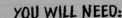

BRILLIANT BIRTHDAY CARDS

When you make your own birthday cards, you can personalize them for the lucky recipient.

1 For the stencil, draw a small, simple outline of a picture on the paper that you can cut out.

2 Cut a straight line to the picture from the edge of the card, then carefully cut the shape out, ending back at the straight line. Tape the paper back together along the cut line, completely covering the cut.

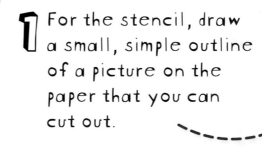

3 Fold the paper for the card in half, then open out flat. Place the stencil on the right half of the card.

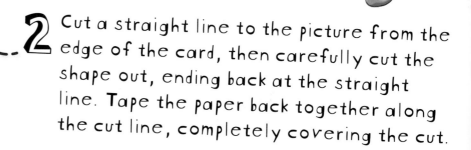

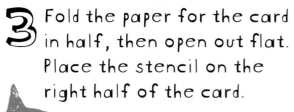
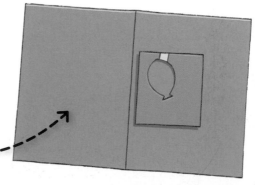

4 Pour a small amount of paint into the plastic cup. Dip the paintbrush into the paint. While holding the stencil down with one hand, tap the brush around the inside and edges of the cutout area. Do this until the whole shape is filled in with paint.

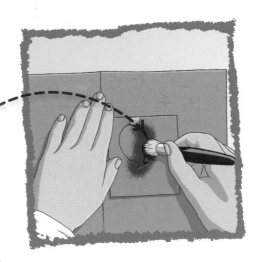

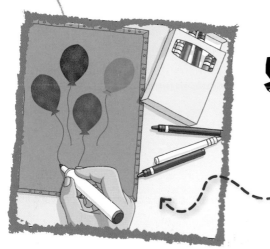

5 Lift the paper stencil off and let the paint dry. Repeat with different colors until you are happy with the design. When the paint is dry, personalize the card with crayons, stickers, marker pens and glitter glue.

happy birthday

happy birthday

The shape cutout of the stencil can be used as a mask. Use it like a stencil, tapping the paint around the edges of the shape.

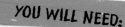

PRINTED GIFT STICKERS

Customize your own gift stickers using floral foam.

1 Draw a simple design onto one side of the floral foam, piercing the surface of the foam with the pencil as you draw. Carve out a rectangular space at the bottom, leaving a border. This will leave a space to write in.

2 Squeeze a small amount of paint onto a sponge, then use your fingers to spread it around the surface. Place a piece of testing paper on top of a folded towel.

3 Press the carved side of the floral foam onto the paint on the sponge, then stamp it onto the test paper. If the design is faint in areas, redraw it into the foam, piercing deeper. Test the stamp again. You might need to do this a few times to get a print you are happy with.

4 Place the label paper on top of the towel. Press the foam onto the paint sponge and stamp onto the label paper. Repeat this until the label paper is covered. Add more paint to the sponge when needed.

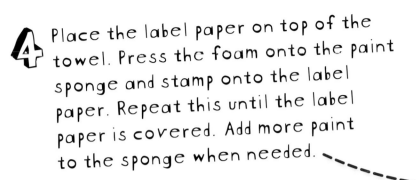

5 Use marker pens to color in the white areas of the stamps. Finally, cut the sheet into individual gift stickers.

Jack   Olivia   Ruby   Thomas

Perfect for Christmas if you need to tag a lot of presents!

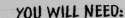

VEGGIE-PRINT BAG

Design your own bag using printing objects from around your home.

YOU WILL NEED:

- Fabric bag
- Cardboard or folded newspaper
- Fruits or vegetables, such as an orange and carrot
- Acrylic paint, in various colors
- Plastic cups
- Sponge brush
- Knife (and an adult to help you!)
- A toy car or other objects from around the home with interesting shapes, textures or patterns

1 Lay the bag flat and put a piece of cardboard or folded newspaper inside it. This will stop the paint from soaking through to the other side. Make sure the bag is smooth and not wrinkled.

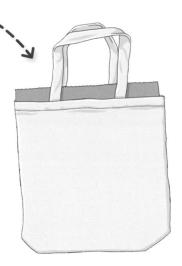

2 Ask an adult to cut some fruits or vegetables in half or into small pieces. Remove any seeds.

3 Squeeze a small amount of paint into a plastic cup. Dip the sponge brush into the paint, then brush it onto the cut side of a piece of fruit or vegetable.

4 Press the fruit or vegetable stamp onto the bag. Continue printing with different pieces and colors, making a picture or design. Let it dry, then print the other side of the bag.

5 With a sponge brush, brush paint onto the wheels of a toy car. Roll the wheels along the fabric to make printed tire tracks. You can use almost any object or toy you like to print with, but remember to ask for permission first!

Don't eat any of the fruits or vegetables that you have painted!

PERSONALIZED STATIONERY

Print your own stationery for letters, thank you notes or invitations!

1 Open the stationery paper and place it flat, with the outside facing up, in the direction you want the card to be. Place the object to be used as a stencil on the half of the card that is the front. Here, a flat plastic animal has been used.

2 Squeeze a small amount of paint into a plastic cup. Dip the paintbrush into the paint. While holding the object on the paper with one hand, tap the brush around the edges of the object and any cut-out areas. Do this until the whole shape is stenciled with paint.

3 After the paint is dry, stencil again on a different area with the same object, or a different one. Use a different color of paint if you like. You can also stencil the half of the card that is the back.

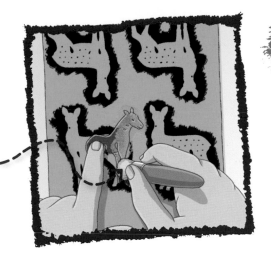

4 You can also try printing the objects instead of stenciling. With a sponge brush, apply paint onto the object. Stamp the object onto the paper, pressing down all of the edges. Repeat as many times as you like.

5 Stencil and stamp the envelope to match.

Be creative—there are loads of colors and designs to choose from.

BUBBLE WAND BOARD

Liven up a plain bulletin board with colorful stenciling.

YOU WILL NEED:

- Acrylic paint, in various colors
- Plastic cups
- Paintbrush or sponge brush
- Cork bulletin board
- Large bubble wand with shapes
- Fat paintbrush
- Paper towel
- Old toothbrush
- Felt-tip pens

1 Squeeze a small amount of paint into a plastic cup. Add a little water to thin the paint and stir. Paint the front and frame of the bulletin board. Let it dry.

2 Squeeze a small amount of a different colored paint into a cup. Place a bubble wand where you want it on the bulletin board. Dip the fat paintbrush into the paint. Hold the bubble wand flat with one hand and tap the brush in all the cut out spaces of the bubble wand.

3 Clean the bubble wand with a damp paper towel. Repeat the previous step, using a different color paint if you like, this time with the wand in another place. Continue stenciling with the same wand, or another one, until you have a design you're happy with. Remember to let the paint dry before stenciling on top of another design.

24

 After the paint is dry, you can add to the design with felt-tip pens.

 To finish, create a splatter pattern. Squeeze a small amount of paint onto an old toothbrush. With the bristles facing down, run your finger across the bristles towards you to splatter paint on the bulletin board.

Use colors to match the colors of your bedroom.

SUPER SKETCHBOOK

Every artist needs a sketchbook. Here's how to make your own!

YOU WILL NEED:

- Scissors
- Cardboard
- Heavy paper for the cover
- White glue in a squeeze bottle
- Crayons
- Paper for inside the book, about 5-8 sheets
- Hole punch
- Ribbon or yarn, three times the length of the book
- Marker pens and glitter glue

1 Cut the cardboard a little smaller than the paper for the cover. Draw any design you like onto the cardboard.

2 Trace over the lines of your picture with white glue and let it dry. The glue should dry in raised, hard lines. This is your rubbing plate.

3 Put the cover paper on top of the rubbing plate. Scribble over it with crayons to make the design appear, filling the whole paper.

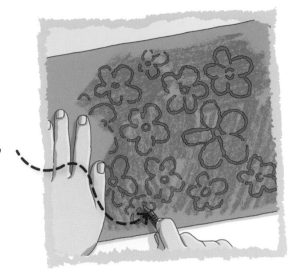

4 Stack the cover and the inside paper together, and fold them in half. Open them back up. Punch a hole about 1 inch from each end on the fold. You will need to punch several sheets at a time instead of all of them together.

5 Stack the cover and pages together again. String the yarn or ribbon through the holes. Tie snugly on the outside to hold the book together. Decorate your sketchbook with marker pens and glitter glue.

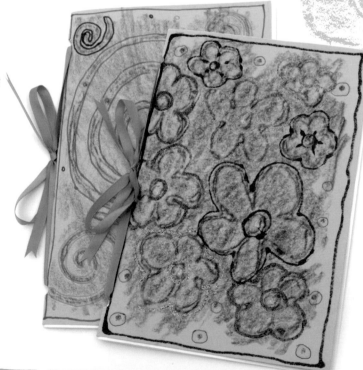

Use lined paper for the inside pages and you can use this book as a journal!

MATERIALS

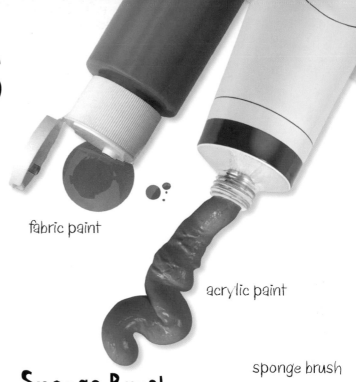

fabric paint

acrylic paint

Paint

When printing on fabric, such as canvas shoes or bags, either fabric paint or acrylic paint can be used. Acrylic paint does not need to be heat set and will dry stiffer than fabric paint. Because of this, it's best to use fabric paint on T-shirts. Some fabric paint need to be heat set with an iron to make them permanent. Follow the directions on the bottle to ensure the paint won't wash out when washed. For projects that are printed on paper, poster paint or acrylic paint can be used.

poster paint

Paint Palette

Paint palettes can be plastic place mats, a piece of acrylic glass, a paper plate or cardboard covered in wax paper. When monoprinting, a piece of acrylic glass will work best for the paint palette.

sponge brush

Sponge Brush

A sponge brush is best when painting onto objects that are to be used to print with, because it will absorb excess paint. Use a sponge brush when the printing object is too large to fit onto a stamp pad.

Adhesive Foam sheets

These are thick sheets of a lightweight but tough, bendy material, that are adhesive on one side. You can cut them into shapes and they bend without tearing.

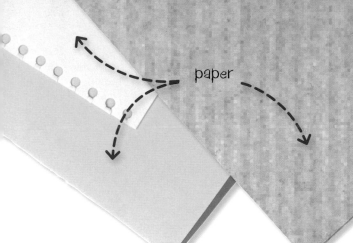

paper

white glue

Paper

Almost any kind of paper can be used with these projects, as long as it can hold up to being painted.

Work Preparation

It's important to cover the work surface with plastic or paper to prevent any permanent accidents and to make cleanup easier. Inexpensive plastic tablecloths work well. Also, wearing an old shirt or an apron is a good idea to protect clothing. Be sure to have some baby wipes or paper towels handy to cleanup any spills or messy hands.

White Glue

White glue is available from all good art and craft shops. It usually comes in a squeeze bottle with a nozzle, which makes it ideal for using to trace designs.

Printing Objects

Almost anything can be used to print with, as long as you ask permission first and it can hold up to being painted. Plastic toys and fruit and vegetables make great printing objects, as does anything with an interesting pattern or texture.

Floral Foam (Oasis)

Floral foam is available from florists and garden centres. It is great to make a stamp from as it is very stiff and easy to carve designs into.

floral foam

foam sheet

TECHNIQUES

Applying Paint

Paint is applied to the stamps and printing tools in different ways, depending on the tool or technique.

A sponge brush is used to apply paint to roller printing tools or to large printing plates. When the stamp is too big for a stamp pad, such as vegetable stamps or toys, a sponge brush is also used. Dip the sponge brush in paint and apply it to the item.

For small or delicate items, like floral foam stamps or modeling clay stamps, press them onto a homemade foam stamp pad to apply the paint. If paint is applied with a sponge brush, it will clog up the carved design lines.

The foam or sponge stamp is dipped into the paint until the bottom surface is covered. A fat paintbrush is used to apply paint for stenciling. Pour a small amount of paint into a plastic cup, dip the brush into the paint, then hold the stencil flat with one hand and tap the brush around the edges and open areas of the stencil. Do this until all of the open spaces of the stencil have been filled in.

Making a Stamp Pad

Some stamps, such as those made from modeling clay or floral foam, work best with a foam stamp pad that you can make yourself. Put a small sponge on top of a plastic lid. (If it's the type of sponge that is hard when dry, wet it first to soften it, then squeeze out all of the water.) Squeeze a small amount of paint onto the sponge, then use your fingers to spread it around. Use it just like a normal stamp pad, but add more paint as needed. Wash out the sponge when you are done.

Stenciling

Stenciling prints the negative spaces of a design. You can either make your own stencils out of paper, or use things like masking tape and stickers. Objects like bubble wands or plastic toys can also be used as stencils. Stencils are great to use when you want to repeat a design for a project.

Gluing

Glue can be used to create a rubbing plate or it can be used to attach thick wool to cardboard to create a printing plate. For a rubbing plate, draw a picture onto a piece of cardboard, then trace over the picture with glue. Once dry, place paper on top of the rubbing plate and scribble over it with crayons to make the design appear. You can use as many colors as you want, overlapping them, or only use one color.

Toothbrush Spatter Paint

Spatter painting with a toothbrush looks like splattered spray paint but uses a toothbrush and paint. Squirt a small amount of paint on an old toothbrush, then with the bristles facing down, run your finger across the bristles toward you to spatter paint on the project. Use several colors for different colored spatters.

Monoprinting

Use this technique when you only want to make one print. It involves drawing directly into the paint on a paint palette. Spread a thin layer of paint onto a paint palette with a sponge brush, then draw a design into the paint with your finger, a paintbrush or the eraser end of a pencil. Remember that everything will print backwards, so if you want any writing, it needs to be backwards too. Place the printed side of the paint palette onto the project, pressing down on it to be sure the whole design prints, then carefully remove it.

INDEX